D0503591

PIONEER EDITION

By Susan E. Goodman and Mimi Mortezai

CONTENTS

Ancient Art

See the wonders of early art.

Easter Island

By Susan E. Goodman

People make art. We have done so for ages. We use art to share our **ideas**. It is part of being human.

No one knows who made the first art objects. Some of the oldest art is from Africa. One **picture** was made 70,000 years ago.

Many people lived in caves then. They hunted animals. They gathered plants. They used stone tools. That time is called the **Stone Age**.

You can find **ancient** art all over the world. People made the art long ago. It tells us about life back then. Let's go see some of it.

Ancient art can raise questions. You'll see that as you read on. Our first stop is England.

Newspaper Rock, Utah

3

Stone Circles

A circle of huge stones stands in England. It is called Stonehenge.

No one knows who built the circle. People once thought giants built it.

Today we know better. Real people built the circle. They started about 5,000 years ago. The work took 2,000 years to finish.

The builders dug a huge circle. It could hold a football field. They placed stones inside the circle. Then they added a ring of giant stones. These stones came from another place. It was 20 miles away. It took 400 builders to move each stone.

What's It For?

Why did people build Stonehenge? No one knows. Maybe it helped them study the sun and other stars.

There is a clue. One stone is called the Heel Stone. It marks times in the year. The sun rises over it on the longest day. The sun sets over it on the shortest day. Maybe Stonehenge is a huge calendar.

Cave Artists

Our next stop is France. Stone Age people lived in caves there. They painted on the walls.

You see wild horses and rhinos on the walls. Those animals no longer live in France.

The artists made their own paint. They used crushed rocks, clay, and water. They made paintbrushes, too.

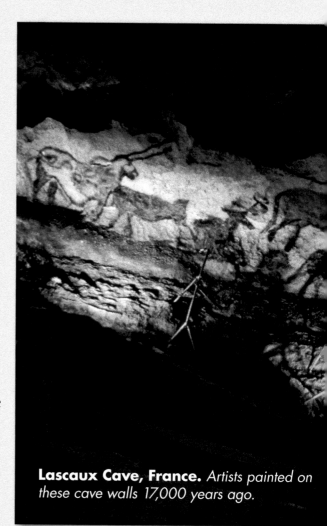

Lascaux Cave, France. *Artists painted on these cave walls 17,000 years ago.*

Stonehenge, England. *Each of these huge stones weighs about 26 tons.*

Easter Island, Pacific Ocean.
Hundreds of giant stones tower over Easter Island. Some are 20 feet tall.

Nazca Lines, Peru.
Why did the Nazca Indians make these huge pictures? No one knows.

Lines in the Sand

Now let's visit Peru. There we find an amazing plain. It is a large, flat area. The plain is covered with art.

Ancient people, called the Nazca Indians, made long lines in the ground. One is more than seven miles long! Some are straight. Others are not. The lines form pictures.

Big Pictures

The pictures are huge. One shows a lizard. It is as big as two football fields. You can also see a monkey and a spider. There are other animals, too.

The Nazca made these animal pictures more than 1,500 years ago. How? They cleared rocks from the plain. The dirt under the rocks was a lighter color. It made the lines stand out.

Why did they make these big pictures? That is a **mystery**.

Land of the Giants

Our last stop is Easter Island. It has hundreds of stone heads. They were made about 1,000 years ago.

Some are 20 feet tall. Some weigh almost as much as 50 elephants! We can only wonder how those stones were moved.

That is one of the secrets to great art. Great art makes us ask questions.

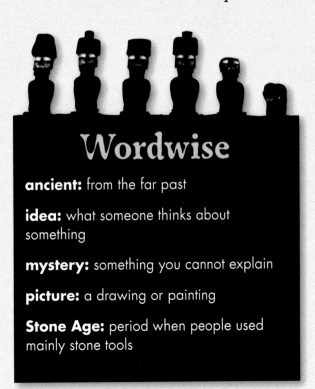

Wordwise

ancient: from the far past

idea: what someone thinks about something

mystery: something you cannot explain

picture: a drawing or painting

Stone Age: period when people used mainly stone tools

Stories in STONE

By Mimi Mortezai

THEY SAY A PICTURE is worth a thousand words. Think of a painting. What does it tell you? Art lets people in every culture "talk" without words. This started thousands of years ago with rock art.

Rock art is a way ancient people shared ideas with each other. People told stories through art. They used rock carvings called petroglyphs. Petroglyphs show messages and ideas. Many scientists study their meaning. Yet most meanings remain a mystery.

Where in the World?

People have made rock art all around the world. Here are a few examples.

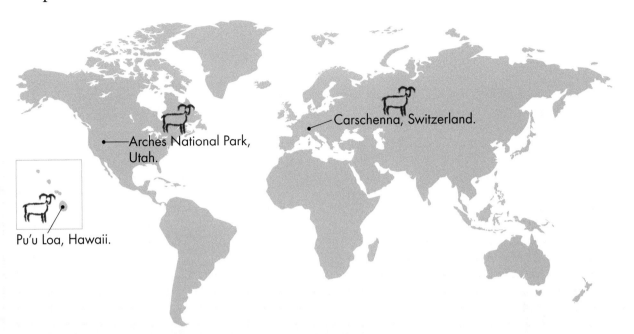

Arches National Park, Utah.

Carschenna, Switzerland.

Pu'u Loa, Hawaii.

Arches National Park, Utah. *Some petroglyphs show familiar ideas. This carving shows hunters and sheep.*

Pu'u Loa, Hawaii. *Families went to Pu'u Loa. They carved petroglyphs to record their visit. A circle with a dot stands for a healthy first child. These carvings show that ancient Hawaiians cared about each other.*

Carschenna, Switzerland. *Other petroglyphs show symbols and mysterious shapes. People think these shapes are maps and trails.*

Computer Connection

What happens when these ancient symbols, or shapes, are connected to cutting-edge computer technology? Discoveries happen.

Computers help people uncover new meanings for ancient symbols. National Geographic Society/Waitt Grantee Eamonn Keogh is a computer scientist. He uses computers to study mosquitos, arrowheads, and more.

Keogh puts large amounts of information into computers. The computers look for patterns, or ways that the shapes are alike. Looking for these patterns is like looking for gold in a mine. It's called data mining.

Keogh uses data mining to compare symbols from many ancient cultures around the world. By finding how the symbols are alike and different, scientists can learn more about ancient people.

Make a Match. *Keogh looks for rock art patterns and repeated shapes.*

Query

not true match

not true match

Query

not true match

Similar Symbols?

Many cultures have a symbol for the sun. Look at each of the shapes. What looks the same? What looks different?

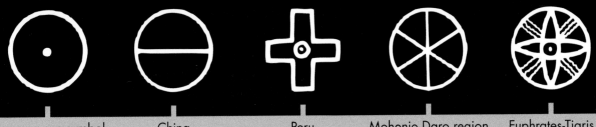

| Common sun symbol found in many cultures | China | Peru, probably Incan | Mohenjo-Daro region (now Pakistan) | Euphrates-Tigris region (now Iraq) |

The Story of Life

Art is important to every culture. It tells the story of its people through pictures. You see their experiences and lives. Pictures show us how cultures are alike. They also show us what makes a culture unique, or special. By comparing images and finding patterns, we can learn a lot about the world and its people. Next time you look at a picture, think about it. What story is it telling you?

What's the Story? *You can tell a lot about a culture when you study its art. What does this picture say?*

11

Art Rocks

Find out what you've learned about ancient art. Then answer these questions.

1 Why did ancient people make art? Why do people study art from long ago?

2 What animals did artists paint on cave walls in France? What did they use to paint them?

3 Imagine you can watch as people make the Nazca Lines. What would you see and feel?

4 What two questions do you have about rock art? Where can you look to find the answers?

5 Why do scientists study symbols that appear in rock art?